Balkan Poetry Today
2017

Balkan Poetry Today

2017

Editor:
Tom Phillips

red hand
BOOKS

First published in 2017 by **Red Hand Books**
part of Red Hand Media Ltd
Flexadux House, Grange Road
Gainsborough DN21 1QB

www.redhandbooks.co.uk

Balkan Poetry Today is published annually by
Red Hand Books, England

This edition: ISBN 978-1-910346-18-1

Prepared for publication by red hand books
Cover design © red hand books

Contents

Editorial

Welcome to the first issue of *Balkan Poetry Today*. We very much hope that you will find it as engaging and interesting to read as it has been to put together. We can't, of course, publish more than a tiny fraction of the work currently being produced across the whole of SE Europe, but we can at least offer a selection that hopefully illustrates its diversity and scope.

Balkan Poetry Today is not designed to be a comprehensive survey. Nor is it a 'greatest hits' package. Not every country in SE Europe, not every language spoken there is represented in this issue (although many are) and readers already familiar with those few poets from the region who have been translated into English may wonder at some of the more notable absences. This, though, is a magazine, not a representative anthology, and our policy has simply been to publish the best work which we have been sent or otherwise come across rather than to fulfil the more ambitious task of charting an entire region's poetic output.

In this first issue, though, you will find a range of both well-established and younger, up-and-coming poets. Some have been translated and published in English – or indeed other languages – before; others haven't. Some have been writing for years and have a long track record of publication; others are still near the beginning of their career. For the most part, we have allowed their poems to speak for themselves, although there is further information about them individually in the 'Notes on contributors' at the back of the issue.

Elsewhere in the magazine, too, you'll find brief introductions to the poets and poetry of particular countries. For *BPT#1*, we have focused on Bulgaria and Macedonia – largely because we happened to receive significant clusters of work from both of them – while in future issues we'll include similar sections on the poetry of other countries and/or languages. Here, too, and by way of introduction to a regular essays and reviews section, you'll find an overview of other recent publications which feature poetry from the Balkans in English translation.

It is, of course, conventional for any publication with the term 'Balkan' in the title to attempt a definition of the region. *BPT* has adopted a rather loose one with blurry edges – and one which includes the various and not-inconsiderable Balkan diasporas. We are, in fact, pretty much leaving it to the poets themselves to decide whether they identify themselves as Balkan or not and to define where the cultural, geographical and linguistic boundaries lie. In practice this means that in this issue you'll find work by a Romanian poet who writes in Czech, a Bulgarian who lives in Slovakia and a Croatian who writes multilingual poems in Croatian, French and English. In future issues we hope to publish work in transnational languages like Roma and Vlach. We use the word 'Balkan' in the broadest possible sense and with no intention of suggesting that 'Balkan poetry' exists as a single, homogenous entity.

Some people, of course, may well question our use of the word 'Balkan' at all. Thanks to derogatory coinages like 'balkanisation' and the apparently relentless stream of negative images about the Balkans which the English-speaking world seems to be particularly adept at producing, *balkanism* has – much like Edward Said's *orientalism* – taken an unfortunate hold. We can't claim, of course, that we're doing anything so grandiose as reclaiming the term, but we can at least say that we're using it in full knowledge of the ways it's been abused as a means of starting to redress the balance and indicate that the Balkans aren't some kind of distant 'other'.

The number of people to whom thanks are due is enormous. Richard Eccles' support for this project has been remarkable from the word 'go' and his agreeing to publish *BPT* under the Red Hand Books imprint means that the magazine now forms part of a portfolio which also includes *Turkish Poetry Today*. I am also deeply indebted to the poets and translators who have responded with such enthusiasm to the idea of publishing a magazine of contemporary Balkan poetry and who have spread the word so effectively. We also very gratefully acknowledge the work of the translators who have sent us work and regret that space has not allowed us to provide more information about them as well as the poets they have translated. In particular I would like to thank Will Firth, Noah Charney, Dimana Ivanova, Alexander Shurbanov, Zvonko Karanovic, Duta Dan Mircea and Silvia Kadiu for putting me in touch with such extraordinarily talented poets from across the whole of SE Europe and helping with the editorial process.

As of September, 2017 *BPT* will be edited from Sofia.

Tom Phillips

With especial thanks to the translators: Zoran Ancevski; Judit Antal; Fadil Bajraj; Elizabeta Bakovska; Suadela Balliu; Alexandra Channer; Andrew K. Davidson; Clifford Endres; Will Firth; Hatto Fischer; Bernie Higgins; Andrea Jurjević; Silvia Kadiu; Iliyana Mircheva; Biljana B. Obradović; Alicia Ostriker; Tsvetomira Peykova; Mary Radosavljević; Lee Schweninger; Nataša Srdić; Igor Stefanovski; Jovana Stojkovska; Katerina Stoykova-Klemer; Henry Taylor; Roumiana Tiholova; Yuliyana Todorova; Galina Tudyk; Suzana Vuljević-Gojçaj; Granit Zela. And, of course, the poets who have translated themselves.

Red Hand Books would like to give a very special thank you to Tom Phillips who brought all of this together and made it happen.

Tom Phillips is the editor of Balkan Poetry Today. He was born in 1964 and is a poet, playwright, translator and lecturer currently living in Bristol, UK. His poetry has been published in a wide range of magazines, anthologies and pamphlets, as well as in the full-length collections *Recreation Ground* (Two Rivers Press, 2012) and *Непознати Преводи/Unknown Translations* (Scalino, 2016). Recent plays include *No Time for Hope* (Ship & Castle, Bristol), *Coastal Defences* (Theatre West, Bristol) and *100 Miles North of Timbuktu* (Theatre West, Bristol). Tom is also the co-founder of *Culture Exchange Experiment* – an informal network of writers and artists in SE Europe and the UK – and of *Colourful Star,* an online project which features his poetry and the paintings of Marina Shiderova. In summer 2016, Tom was a translator-in-residence at the Sofia Literature and Translation House and his translations of contemporary Bulgarian poetry have been published in a number of magazines. Tom has a PhD in creative writing from the University of Reading and has taught creative writing at the universities of Reading and Bath Spa. He has written about SE Europe for academic publications and spoken at international conferences on the representation of the region in English literature. Ian Brinton described *Unknown Translations* as "refreshingly original" while David Cooke called *Recreation Ground* "work of the highest order".

I Poetry from Bulgaria

This section brings together 24 poems by eight poets whose work reflects, but certainly doesn't exhaust the wide spectrum of poetry currently being written and published in Bulgaria. Although all but one of them live and work in Sofia, these poets range in age from their 20s to their 70s and cannot be said to represent any particular generation or 'school'. Nor would it be wise to attempt to identify any stylistic traits or thematic concerns which they all share. Each has his or her own distinctive approach to poetry and, of course, his or her own distinctive voice.

Of these eight, perhaps the most well-known outside Eastern/South Eastern Europe are Aksinia Mihaylova, Vladimir Levchev and Petar Tchouhov. Mihaylova won the 2014 Prix Guillaume Apollinaire for her book of poems in French, *Ciel à Perdre*, while, having previously lived in the US, Levchev has published a number of books there, including 2004's *Black Book of the Endangered Species*. Tchouhov, meanwhile, is an internationally recognised haikuist who has read his work at numerous events and festivals around the globe and features in Shearsman's 2012 anthology of Bulgarian poetry *At the End of the World*.

Also translated and published internationally, Alexander Shurbanov is a respected poet and a highly regarded translator who has translated – amongst others – Chaucer, Shakespeare, Milton and Coleridge into Bulgarian. His recent publications include the poetry collection *Foresun*, which gathers together poems from across his career rendered into English by himself and others – two of which are published here. Dimana Ivanova is another poet-translator. She currently lives and works in Slovakia but has published two books of poetry in Bulgaria including last year's *Alphabet of the Desires*, from which the three poems translated here are taken.

Amelia Licheva, on the other hand, is a distinguished literary theorist and the editor of Bulgaria's principal literary newspaper, *Литературен вестник* – a publication which reflects the centrality of writing to the country's culture – while Mila Lambovska is a consulting psychologist whose most recent poetry collection, *Годината на Джорджа* (*The Year of Georgia*) reflects her interest in both psychology and the possibilities of language.

The youngest poet here is Iliyan Lyubomirov. Now aged 27, he has published two collections of poetry, the first of which, *Нощта е Действие* (*The Night is Action*), became the fastest-selling book of poetry to have been published in Bulgaria since the end of communism in 1989 and sold more than 4,000 copies within days of its publication. Again the three poems published here are taken from that book and exemplify its key themes – the life of a young metropolitan in a fast-changing city whose roots extend back to the more traditional culture of rural Bulgaria.

As with the magazine as a whole, this section can't pretend to do more than represent a small sample of contemporary Bulgarian poetry. Other Bulgarian poets will, of course, feature in future issues, but we hope that this selection will at least serve as a taster of the poetry itself and of the passion with which it is being written and disseminated.

Tom Phillips

Alexander Shurbanov

Three picture poems

1. Vermeer's milkmaid

The arms – strong, clean –
are bared up to the elbows.
One hand props
the earthen jug from below,
the other holds it firmly
from above,
tilting it slightly
over a bowl
placed on the table
between a round loaf
in the bread-basket
and a bulging pitcher.
A thin trickle of milk
stretches from the jug
to the bowl,
tying the whole picture
together.
On the left is the window.
The young woman's head
is slightly tilted
over the shoulder,
the hair is pulled under
the starched Dutch bonnet
with one wing pressed tight
and the other a little spread out.
The eyes, downcast,
watch the milk
as it keeps flowing.
Isn't this power of art
truly wonderful?
Centuries pass
by the earthen jug
as it tilts over the bowl
at an unchanged angle,
wars rage around,
cities are consumed by fire,
ships sink
and planes crash to the ground,
regimes, states, nations, philosophies

come and go,
the world becomes new,
changing out of recognition.
Yet this thin white trickle of milk
keeps flowing
from the jug into the bowl,
and the jug is still full,
and the face
of the unaging young woman
overflows with calm.

Translated by the author

2. And what if we suppose ...

*A footnote to what W.H. Auden and William Carlos Williams say
regarding Pieter Bruegel's picture 'Landscape with the Fall of Icarus'*

Yet if we suppose
that none but us, staring at this picture
(and the artist, of course),
could see the disappearance in the water
of one folded bare leg and one outstretched
(undoubtedly belonging to the boy fallen from the skies) –

If we suppose
that neither the ploughman pushing the plough,
nor the shepherd, his back to the sea,
nor any of his sheep,
nor even the crew of the exquisite ship,
sliding so gracefully so close
to the drowning boy,
nor either the man leaning towards him from the shore
(if the red hat doesn't reveal
that that is actually the artist himself
and therefore different from the others,
rather than a mere fisherman,
intent on his task) –

None of these
has been able to hear the splash
of the falling body,
and see its tumultuous submergence into the water,

If we only suppose, I say –
'cause maybe it's exactly what
the creator of this diminutive world
within the frame of the picture
was trying to do:
to show simultaneously
in a single space
two incompatible realities –
the one on this side, familiar to everyone,
and another one
that can sometimes be glimpsed along its edge –
that other one
that holds no ploughmen, shepherds, fishermen
and speeding boats,
but only monsters with huge horned heads

on human trunks,
magical labyrinths and towers,
and youths flying up to the sun
on their impossible wings of wax,

If we suppose...

Then who would've known
that somewhere there could exist an Icarus;
who could've seen and heard him with his this-side senses?
And if someone really
managed to break the mental wall
and reach out to pull him out of the water
and save him
from his doomed,
repeatedly re-written
and therefore inconclusive death;
would not this somebody
kill him off in the act once and for all,
just as Bruegel's fisherman
would kill his fish,
if he were allowed to pull it out
into our air?

Translated by Yuliyana Todorova

3. Imitation

This is the picture
of an unknown
eighteenth-century painter –
apparently Hungarian.
It is in fact
the family portrait
of a jeweller
and his son
at a workbench
displaying
a neat array of instruments –
pincers, files, fine saws,
vices and magnifying lenses –
all of them apparently real,
drawn to the last detail.
The jeweller
is smartly dressed –
as for a photo.
His eyes,
brown and intelligent,
thoughtful,
seem to be looking at you
through time.
The slender fingers
are holding what appears
to be a brooch,
probably just perfected.
The man seems to have been
proud of his art
and satisfied with himself.
Where can these eyes,
these gentle fingers
be now,
two hundred years later?
Even the name of the jeweller –
like that of the painter –
has been forgotten.
The boy
looks like him –
with a kind face
and smoothed hair.
Did he learn
his father's craft?
Was he as successful in life

as his father?
And does anyone know
where he is buried?
He looks so keenly alive!
The playful eyes
are half-smiling
at somebody
diagonally in front of the painting –
probably his mother.
Not even her likeness
has been preserved.

Translated by the author

'Vermeer's Milkmaid' and 'And What If We Suppose...' appear in the author's recent book of poems in translation *Foresun* (Sofia: Scalino, 2016).

Aksinia Mihaylova

Private lessons in May

I'm trying to teach you the Cyrillic alphabet of scents:
that the geranium on the balcony across the street
is more than a mere geranium,
that the linden tree in June
is more than a mere tree,
but we aren't making progress fast enough.
Your thumb is following the candle shadow
that the wind is making tremble on the open page,
as if drafting mobile borders
between you and me,
as if to protect you,
as if you are that boy,
who once lost his watercolours
on his way home from school,
and who's still painting
the lost sky of his childhood and the hills
in the same colour.

Translated by Roumiana Tiholova

Passing trains

To my brother

Everything is still the same
after the midpoint of our lives just passed –
we buy apples
at the market next to the train station,
a kilogram of corn seeds to be sown by our father,
some seedlings of petunias for our mother.
Fifteen minutes embrace
a few Saturdays spent together
at different platforms.
And as we're stirring up our silence
at the bottom of the plastic coffee cups,
the petunias bloom
as big as the bells of the village church
and start tolling above the roofs,
twice for mama, thrice for papa,
corn is rising into the sky,
where a tired boat
struggles to tear down
the chain of clouds.

When you embrace me
before saying goodbye,
in the fading blue
of your eyes I read with hesitation
that nothing
except our blood
is still the same.

Translated by Roumiana Tiholova

The navel of the world

Where did this mid-May snow in Sarajevo come from?
It looks as though the weather is acquiring people's bad habits.
Everything in history repeats, say the men at the pub.
The Balkans are a swollen vein
which Europe slices open every few decades
to purify its aging blood.
The most important things start at the market,
at the beginning and the end of the century,
every time at a restless market.
Just like spring,
which always comes on a Friday
and chooses a pub with round tables
where the meaning of each unsaid word
is visible from all sides,
just like our innocent hands
in the middle of the table,
shielding the navel of the world.

Translated by Katerina Stoykova-Klemer

Vladimir Levchev

The Balkan bridge

For Ismail Kadare

For millennia we have quarrelled,
for millennia we have built and demolished
the Balkan bridge
(over the Drina,
over the Danube,
over the Ujana e Keqe
in Albania)...

For millennia we have asked ourselves:
Where is the Golden City – East
or West?
Where is the real Prophet?
And what will be our profit
from that bridge
between the Sunrise and the Sunset?

With knives in our teeth,
we have asked ourselves:
Is it true that living people,
our people,
have been immured
to make the bridge stronger?

For millennia we have quarrelled, and fought,
died and killed,
built and demolished...

Meanwhile
the airlines were invented.
Today no traveller can see
our ancient bridge.

Translated by the author with Alicia Ostriker

The Balkan dance

We are the soldiers of king Samuil
blinded by Basil,
the emperor of Constantinople.
We are fifteen thousand men.
One in every ten of us
has one eye to lead us.
We hold hands, walk and trip,
like a ring dance
from horizon to horizon
under the light of the sunset.
We were returning home
to our king Samuil.
The king saw us
and died of a heart attack.
But we didn't see him.
So we continue our dance
barefooted in wild forests,
on the embers of camp fires,
sliding on frozen lakes
under the cold sharp constellations...

We are dancing towards a new millennium
and all we can see
in our future
is our past.

Translated by the author with Henry Taylor

Five years after 9/11

For Raina

It's been like in those dreams:
you are at the beach,
in August, in high school,
green airy waves and laughter
of girls and seagulls.
And the snow begins to fall:
slow letters and shirts
from a heavenly explosion.
And the smiling faces
of teachers and kids
morph into monsters.
Later black kites and ravens
fly by low
over the leaden ocean.
And you realize
that your dream has come true:
you have grown up.
And you can't wake up anymore
in that warm
other country.

Washington, DC, 9/11/2006

Written in English

Petar Tchouhov

Softly

I know dangerously little
about love

Even though I've taken her
to the movies
removed
her shades
put gifts
beneath her pillow

Once I lived with her
for two whole years
in a birdhouse
but she flew off

Even so I think
we were closest
that night
when I dreamt of her
with my head
on the fur
of a dog
which wasn't
even mine

Translated by Tom Phillips

Choice

I want to stand
on the right side
of the camera

on such things depend
whether her face will be in the sun
for the next couple of decades

whether her smile will take to the wind
that plays with her skirt
or stay as warm
as a house cat
at arm's length

whether the gesture with which she fixes her hair
will fall from the book which I'm reading
in the evening before I go to sleep

or sometime when my eyes fade
like batteries
I'll think God who has seen me
so beautiful

Translated by Tom Phillips

Steampunk

The buffalos are sitting
in the meadow by the village
history's
abandoned locomotives

An old man
and an old woman
quarrel in the yard
of the last house
beside the remains of their love –
a rusty Moskvitch
that long ago stopped
moving

From its nest on the roof
a stork lifts off
like a stream of smoke
above a ship

The granddaughter peeks
sleepily through the window
takes a sip of coffee
the colour of petrol
lights her first cigarette
of the day

and slowly begins
to peel
a clockwork apple

Translated by Tom Phillips

Iliyan Lyubomirov

Constancy kills

colours are inconstant
as you
take lilacs
their purple will fade
will turn into the white
of the lily of the valley's iris
the tulip's ruddiness
will leave just like yours
and will lodge in a clump
of poppies on some shore
to wait for those selfsame sunsets
in which
the green of the grass
will become the pallor
of your dishevelled hair

Translated by Iliyana Mircheva, Tsvetomira Peykova and Tom Phillips

in the hoarfrost out in the yard
grandma would have found
quinces and medlars
already perished
without an ounce
of a pomegranate's pretence
she would've taken them
in her apron pocket
to warm them up
she could have boiled them
into a compote or jam
she could have left them
in the basket with the oranges
so they too might rub shoulders
with some distant exotica

yes, but grandma is gone
and there are no oranges in the basket
and grandpa has nothing left to do
except to boil the quinces
for rakiya
and drink alone
next to the cooking stove
already growing cold

Translated by Iliyana Mircheva, Tsvetomira Peykova and Tom Phillips

Dress code

for every new man
you buy yourself a dress
and I've already lost track
of which is mine
and how many are crammed
in your wardrobe

in the morning you always sit
on the edge of the bed
with your back to me
head bowed
and hair gathered up

and I have no strength
for anything except
pulling up the zip
of your new dress

Translated by Iliyana Mircheva, Tsvetomira Peykova and Tom Phillips

Dimana Ivanova

Allegory

In one dead square
of this wholly forgotten palace,
I saw a crowd of shadowy figures
reaching out to the coach
in which Ignorance sat,
shameless, inglorious,
vain,
Kafka, Beckett, Herbert are dead,
Botev, Yavorov, Debelyanov are dead,
two sad silver horses pulled her carriage,
it's cold in this palace
of death,
even the figures who crowned her are soulless.
Grey
mists dance around a black sun –
there's no hope
of revival.

Translated by Tom Phillips

Queen Elizabeth I

In the gloom of old London,
in a sad but frivolous world,
the queen remains behind
the palace's impregnable walls –
beautiful, intelligent, cold.
Elizabeth, bold, daring queen of England and Ireland,
ghosts and demons wrap you in an enchanted veil.

Heads bow before your might –
actors, poets, artists, envoys, mummers, magi –
but beside your regal path
an ominous grey sorrow lurks in blue shadows.

Shakespeare's tragic ghosts guard you.
And time protects you –
watching like a huge lion, a mute page,
ready to leap on your enemies
with terrible force.

Translated by Tom Phillips

(Un)Known

He is the known-unknown,
he often travels
on the 37 bus.
He always gets off
at Kerepuski.
He is the man
who stands in the back row
of the audience
at my book launch
and smiles enigmatically.
Then he says: "You don't
look like a Bulgarian woman.
You don't have a Bulgarian soul."
And he disappears.
He is the man – a connoisseur,
a seeker after the female spirit.
You can see him
in the Art Forum bookshop on Kozya Street.
He goes in and takes a book, here he is again –
he opens it, he reads, he smiles
enigmatically ... he leaves it and takes another.
Then another and another...
Then he goes out and loses himself
in the city's embrace.
And visibly anxious
I head for the bookshelf
whose bodies the known-unknown was holding.
Mila Haugova,
Vera Prokeshova,
Stanislava Repar –
female pens
with a fierce hold
in literature's flesh.

Translated by Tom Phillips

Mila Lambovska

Goggling fish head

It strikes me
at the harbour's far end
between the old yachts
and the makeshift fish market
surrounded
by bad dogs and mangy cats

I recognise it
by its hooligan look
its brash sexuality
bumptious crude

It's a verse from another poem
a fragment
left by other devastating storms
on the shore
of other islands

Translated by Tom Phillips

Andemo da Florian

the calm waters at sunset
leaf through *Corriere della sera*
men avidly read
each passing woman
the lagoon satisfies its fantasies
about the tourists
the changes would be marginal
if we went back to February 1760
when Count Gozzi took to
writing gossip columns and founded
Gazetta Veneta

Translated by Tom Phillips

Your name

it hatches in a cuckoo's nest

Your name is meaningless
however it's written
Your name is a tired sea
with no emotional connection
to the dead cat and the evergreen
ivy leaves,
nor the silent island in the dregs of the cup
of Turkish coffee

You're looking for logic in the lines
of this poem but it lacks so much as a kiss
so much as a chessboard where,
in the black D4 square, I could lay the cat to rest

An old Bedouin
staring at his reflection in the entrance
of an ultramodern hotel in Riyadh
will carefully write
your name in Arabic
The desert will pretend
that it can't read

Translated by the author and Tom Phillips

Amelia Licheva

Girlfriends

When she goes into the classroom
and flicks her hair
and provocatively crosses her legs
and pulls on her neckline
and shakes her newly formed breasts
and smiles with her reddened lips
and blinks with her mascara'd eyes
and stretches her body
on which hang and jingle
jewellery, bands, frills
and every kind of small and tempting thing,
the eyes of my classmates shine,
and their faces reveal
how the story
of their fathers and mothers,
their grandpas and grandmas
is projected on them,
the story of heroes
who dream
of being,
the story
which they want to make...

Translated by Tom Phillips

Sometimes...
my great-grandfather
sent a postcard
of the Prater
from Vienna
and wrote:
"You have to see this!"
And my mother,
who didn't keep the card
but remembers the story
and remembers her dream
of Vienna
tells me about this city
at the heart of Europe
which I have to see

in a new century
I'm strolling
through a big park,
beside shooting galleries,
merry-go-rounds
and kiosks selling candyfloss
it's not so different
from Sofia
and Boris Gardens in my childhood
the titbits taste the same
only there are more languages
and the merriment is more authentic

but when I ride the big wheel
and see Vienna beneath my feet
I understand
what my great-grandfather wrote and why

Translated by Tom Phillips

Where is Europe?

On the flight
which slowly takes you away
from the familiar speech at the airport,
where there's no way not to feel
cosmopolitan,
especially if you're flying on some unknown flight
from some unknown country,
at the airport
where you're like everyone,
because Schengen is a memory,
is this Europe?
the place to which you're heading,
the dream which you hold
the history which you know
the pictures which your eyes painted...
or Europe is arriving,
checking there's conformity
between sleep and waking
between object and photo
and maybe Europe
is the little souvenirs
you buy
below the Eiffel Tower
outside Notre Dame,
beside Strasbourg cathedral,
beside the cathedral in Cologne,
in the square in Rome...
Europe is a tourist attraction –
you hand over a ticket and watch
the 12 apostles pass in front of your eyes,
how the hourglass measures time,
you turn your head left and right,
right and left,
so as to remember
at least for a short while
that house and that palace
and that stone
what they are, what they have been,
who brought them to life.
You take a boat along the Seine and Rhine,
you prise out a souvenir of Metz's yellow stone
or the rosy stone of Strasbourg
you take away the thought of a shop window,

of an organ playing,
of the woman
who saw you wandering around Montmartre
and ran towards you
so as to trace the path on the map

on this map
on which
you collect parts of Europe.

Translated by Tom Phillips

II Poetry

Stevan Tontić

The event

In the besieged city,
After three months of fear about sheer survival,
Of running from bed to the bomb shelter, of starvation,
Wrested the woman – the Almighty must have given her
                              the signal – one night,
During sunrise, just when the cocks started to crow,
From the body of the man a burst of happiness and bliss,
Wrested it with electrified fingertips and fell asleep
As one of the blessed.

The man stood up,
Bathed ceremoniously by candle light,
Lit himself ceremoniously the last cigarette
And thought not without a certain satisfaction
That the machine of his body could still be used
And the matter, out of which it is composed, does not belong
                              entirely to dust,
Rather that his life makes equally, so to speak,
Here and there some sense.

Translated by Hatto Fischer

Black dog

Into our entry, in flight with his Macedonian master,
Came the black dog,
Strong as a wolf,
Meek as a lamb.

With shells falling all around
The black dog chases over the grass
Free and fearless as a demon,
Happy to run until he drops:
Everytime, with no exception
He fetches the ball his master throws,
Fetches it for us too,
And we keep him running.

As the ball flies farther and farther,
The dog runs faster and faster,
Pants louder and louder
His great tongue lolling to the ground.

I watch the black dog with its laboured breathing,
I watch this black freedom
I watch for the time he collapses
At our feet, feet which never budge
From our sheltering wall.

Translated by Mary Radosavljević

Trip to Paris

Several of us so-called artists
So-called intellectuals
From so-called Bosnia & Hercegovina,
From a city in the darkened heart of this so-called civil war,
One so-called, quite fantastic day, received
An invivation from a so-called European Civil Forum
To attend a certain important meeting
In so-called France.

To leave for Paris
Would be a journey to eternity
A trip to paradise.

A seven-day wait, all present,
Problems with the so-called UN peace force
And the so-called civil authorities
Only to be informed that the trip
To so-called Europe
Had come to nothing.

Because I had been so long away from home
My wife welcomed me as if I had
Really been on a long journey;
She – the only one not so-called –
Was almost ashamed in case the neighbours found out
I had quickly and with such disdain left Paris
To return to this place of unavoidable death.

Translated by Mary Radosavljević

Neşe Yaşın

Camera obscura

Not seen in the photo is
what's passing through you
the letter you wrote just before
my shadow oozing into your gaze
my ghost at the table
the shattering of memory
the heart's trembling poem
the miracle of our night

The rose heartbroken by your smile
your hand reaching for my bitter dream
our hearts hidden in your mind

What's reflected is a moment of illusion
my delicate disaster scattered to the winds
the racing heart makes me dizzy

It's the woman absent from the photo
who leaves a thread of passion in the maze

The true story escapes its reflection
the shot is an undetected crime
there are seven mistakes in this picture

Translated by Clifford Endres

Poison apple

Once I didn't then I did exist
loneliness was my cradle
forgotten in the wind

Pearls ornamented my coverlet
evil-eye beads
frozen in stone gazed at me

When my mother loosed from her hand
birds gave me wings
the trees a nest

It was night
leaf on leaf the forest wept
wolves gave me their breasts

I had a step-god
He would not hear what I said

When I bit into the poison apple
my mother and my love deserted me
I was a branch crying in the frost
water imbibing solitude
the voice of leaves rustling

My lover did or didn't exist
his name was wind, his memory a fish
if I cried he would not
if I explained he would not hear

When I spoke I didn't recognize
my own silent voice
yet one day I solved
the riddle of my wounded soul

Open the door of my heart's secret museum
a girl child hides inside
every heartbroken woman's voice

Its bleeding country records
the fate of every lost love

Time is the eye of the storm
amid the delirium
of demolition

Translated by Clifford Endres

Marija Knežević

Attention

I bought myself a dark blue rose.
Chinese. Made of wood resembling paper.
It is beautiful, it is indeed.
I bought it for myself.
My love was somewhere
thinking calculating weighing
whether this love was worthwhile.

The day was nice but subdued,
like people before the rain.
I had wine and salad for lunch. I took a nap.
And I thought of ordinary things
although I had a dream of something
dreadful, with fire, a terror, a final ending.
It was convincing.
I would say we were all burnt out,
and singing afterwards.

But I am not sure.
That's how I wake up.

Translated by the author

The last lesson in tenderness

When I die,
you must make sure the window is open.
I want to continue to be a landscape
in which we are walking together
our steps joined together
like an undiscovered little animal
taking a stroll
from one species into another.

And make sure the record player is on.
I don't like tango on tapes,
even less the perfection of compact discs.
I want to dance with you in peace
in my thoughts
that dance which can dance with itself.
Find me a record that crackles.
I love to make love to noise.

Open to me all your letters.
I long to sniff them,
the way I've always read them.

At the table, by my bedside,
which was always a deathbed too,
put a shell and a small scented candle.
If you could find the flavour of vanilla,
you'll do me a great favour.

If you translate the imperative
into the language of a wish
that doesn't wish to be fulfilled,
I will let you have my dog.
When you think that I am gone,
if you don't question the origin
of my requests

I will love you more
than alive.

Translated by the author

Ragip Sylaj

A letter to an artist

You're selling cheap the blood of words
While you're squeezing your heart
To bleed the nectar

But why is your sublime love
Furrowed by claws of fear

Its head raised devilishly
When Zeuses watch over you

But freedom costs a lot
And when you survive

All your heritage is pain
And the biggest reward remains

The art of sacrifice –
A testament for an unknown friend

The rider of the dawn would never stop
Wandering through hell
Dreaming through heaven

Face to face with yourself
You'd know the unknown
The mystery of suffering

Then raise the price to the art of love
When demons flirt with muses

Translated by Fadil Bajraj

Anti-hymn for freedom

Freedom is afraid of the people
When its merchants go to the black market

The merchants of freedom at the black market
Are bargaining with our fate

The people are afraid of freedom
Because they still don't know whether they've paid its taxes

The people are afraid of being left in darkness
Because the taxman can expel them from freedom's hour

The citizens don't know that it can't be bought on credit at the supermarket
Nor borrowed from the bank
It is the suicide of fear's cop

It is the unwritten contract with angels
With the predecessors under (mother) ground

"If freedom is afraid of you
If you are afraid of freedom
We are ruined monuments
We are perverted monuments"
The voices from underground scream

Don't censor the sun
Don't increase the dark clouds in eternal heaven
Because dawn's scions pull out the sun from the heart
And they don't allow freedom to walk on crutches

It is not a forbidden fruit from Eden
The Fruit of Life has the same high price as pain itself

As the jewelled pain that saints kiss
As heaven's miracle that came down to earth

A Kosova punished by dreamy happiness
A blessed happiness with a real Kosova

But freedom
What's the price of freedom when you stay alive

Translated by Fadil Bajraj

Jasmina Bolfek-Radovani

Rescue, breathe

The quiet hour
seagulls are hungry
waves are breaking
under their own
froth of saliva

We walk
hand in hand
drawing behind
us the years we spent
together on the sand
of the Adriatic

Our love seems
a long succession
of moments
the glow
and the sorrow
are gone

You say
"Take a stand"
I say
"Understand"

Naked past
conversations
merge into
a soundless
undercurrent
of memories

You say
"Show me
your teeth"
I say
"Breathe"

Round, infinity

On zrači zrakama
mjeseca
Kad gleda u nju,
 When he looks at her,

  Quand il la regarde,

U njenom oku
ogleda se njegovo
jezero dana, noći,

 in his eye, his lake of the day, night,

  *dans son oeil est reflété
  son lac du jour, la nuit,*

Kad govori,
On niže riječi-bisere,
 When he speaks,
 his threads, words-pearls,

  *Quand il parle,
  il tisse des mots-perles,*

ona ih prihvaća,

 she catches them,
  elle les attrape,

U padanju snova,

 In the falling of dreams,

  Dans la chute des rêves,

poput kiše

koja lagano rosi
njenu kožu,

> like raindrops
> landing on her skin,
>> *comme des gouttes d'eau*

>> *tombant sur sa peau,*

kap zastaje
na njenom dlanu,

zavlači se u nju,
puni tamninu

njenog oka

> slowly crawling
> into her,

> filling the darkness
> of her eye
>> *s'introduisent, doucement,*

>> *en elle,*
>> *remplissant la noirceur*
>> *de son oeil,*

koje se ogleda
u njemu dok

gleda u nju.

> reflected
> in his gaze,
>> *reflétées dans son*

>> *regard*

III Poetry from Macedonia

Poetry from Macedonia

Although its 1991 departure from Yugoslavia was peaceful and it avoided the bitter wars which afflicted other former Yugoslav republics, Macedonia's subsequent history has not been untroubled. The 1999 conflict in Kosova saw it having to deal with an influx of more than 350,000 refugees while, in 2001, fighting did break out during an insurgency by Macedonia's Albanian population and led to intervention by NATO. Then there is the long-running dispute with Greece over the country's name which has resulted in international bodies referring to it by the provisional-sounding and rather cumbersome alternative, FYROM or the Former Yugoslav Republic of Macedonia. More recently, both the government and the president have been the focus of popular protests and journalists in SE Europe have drawn attention to a lack of press freedom and to other human rights abuses.

At the same time, Macedonia has a deep-rooted literary culture and is home to one of the biggest poetry festivals in SE Europe – Struga Poetry Evenings. These began in 1961 and have been running annually ever since, recognising poets from around the world with the Golden Wreath award whose recipients include Auden, Ginsberg, Neruda, Heaney and Tranströmer. Arc's 2011 anthology *Six Macedonian Poets* – which includes work by Jovica Ivanovski and Elizabeta Bakovska, who appear here as a poet and translator pairing – has also helped to bring Macedonian poetry to the English-speaking world.

As it happens, three of the poets featured here are part of the Macedonian diaspora. Both Ivan Trposki and Dušan Ristevski migrated to Australia in the 1960s and 1970s and are active in the Macedonian Literary Association 'Grigor Prlichev' there, while Zvonko Taneski currently lives and works in Slovakia but continues to publish his poetry in his native Macedonia. Jovica Ivanovski lives and works in Skopje where his first poetry collection appeared in 1995 and has been followed by a series of critically acclaimed volumes, including two of poems selected from across his career.

The youngest of the Macedonian poets here is Darko Leshoski who was born in Struga – or "the so-called city of poetry" as he likes to call it – in 1984. Like the young Bulgarian poet Iliyan Lyubomirov, he began by publishing his work on the internet, which resulted in his first printed collection selling out on the day of its official launch in 2013. The poem printed here – *'Things worth living for, that I never read about in any damn textbook'* – is both a celebration and a cri de coeur, a contemporary Macedonian response to Ginsberg's *Howl*.

Tom Phillips

Ivan Trposki

Repentance

I wasn't drunk or being stupid
when I promised you I'd return –
you'd only be waiting two years
like the length of military service
two cycles of the grapevine
or until a child is up and walking,
that's all, no longer –
I told you.

You cried
your tears soaked my shirt
you didn't believe my words.

I laughed like a child back then –
back then, fifteen years ago –
but not now.

Translated by Will Firth

There is a journey

There is a journey of darkness and dismay
A cursed journey to wrench a mother's heart.
There is a journey that takes me away – one-way,
A journey at the mercy of the captain's chart.

There is a journey over abyssal depths of the sea
and over eighty million human paces, fleeing.
There is a journey, sickeningly long, from quay to distant quay
that unleashes a war inside, in my very being.

There is an unforgotten journey –
one with a wooden suitcase,
passport and visa
and a youthful face.

Translated by Will Firth

Craft

Before he started the 'ploughing'
my father rolled up his sleeves
knelt before the fecund vale
and bowed as if before an icon
my mother was always waiting to be furrowed
and slowly put her breasts in his hands
so he would keep his balance while ploughing
it was a miracle
that the milk in mother's breasts sufficed
to feed him as well as us
during this everyday ritual
my father and the plough grew in size
while my mother and her field diminished
after the ritual the dimensions changed back
the game lasted until the plough was dented
and the furrowed field exhausted
a splendid craft, absolutely –
the first to be learned and the last to be forgotten

Translated by Will Firth

Jovica Ivanovski

I couldn't find your grave

I couldn't find your grave
in the marble forest.
After the funeral I looked for signs
to get by when I
come for a chat,
but I remembered nothing.
Fifteen minutes from one grave to another
my shoes heavy with mud,
my head with names and faces,
unknown even when they were alive.
I was lost in the labyrinth where
we'll all get lost one day
(or maybe find our place there).
When I came to visit you two years ago
in your new flat, you waited
on the balcony and threw me the key.
Now there's nothing, dead silence
on the lifeless street.
I left feeling guilty
leaving the candles and the flowers
at an unknown grave.
I'll come in the spring,
on a nice sunny day,
with a bottle of Jameson and two
packs of cigarettes,
and I'll sit till they close.

Or maybe the graveyards
work around the clock,
24 hours per day?

Translated by Elizabeta Bakovska

Life in flip-flops

The beach shows the sea its tongue.
The obligations are dogs unleashed.
Sand and hot feet.
The book reads itself,
again and again.
The umbrella planted in the sand
spitefully resists the wind.
The view and the endlessness,
the perspective and you.
A meek sunset and
sourdough Moon.
You are the boss of your peace,
the owner of the present.
A quiet breeze rambles through your hair,
as your mother once did
when she checked
if you got any lice.

Translated by Elizabeta Bakovska

Telephone book

Another anachronism
stored in the basement immediately above
          the Marxism lesson book

once a communication Bible
        thicker than the Old Testament
it ended without glory – with a cross over its forehead

the index finger licks the tongue
it turns pages faster than Google
and searches with its sharp nail as
          with a mouse's arrow

at the time when 988 (because of operator
capacity) was impossible to get
only it memorized the numbers of girls

it was destroyed by mobile phones
just like steam locomotion
        destroyed the post carriage

it only exists in phone booths
           in the American movies
where guys with poor memory tear out
a whole street for a single number

nobody reads it anymore that's why it's not printed
actually it has long experienced
the fate of my poetry

Translated by Elizabeta Bakovska

Dušan Ristevski

Remembrance

Blagoja 'Bill' Neshkovski (24.11.1992)

One November night
balmy and velvet
a white dove
took flight on silent wings
and vanished among the stars.

His mother donned the black of mourning
heavy tears fell
and sighs of silent misfortune;
if only this, if only that, his sisters wished...
his father froze
– his heart stricken.

His native Opticians
were left to pine
in the wilds of Pelagonia
while in Port Kembla,
beneath the smokestacks
of the Steelworks,
the last curtain fell
and he entered the eternal dream
of the Macedonian Shakespeare.

Translated by Will Firth

Bill was born in Optichari, a village near Bitola, whose name literally means 'opticians'.

Empty house

In the distance a church bell rings

An aching and a longing lurk
over the windows and the door

The silhouette of a woman
a smiling face
forced to don the black of mourning

In the distance a church bell rings

The wall is cracked
the plaster crumbles
the wind bangs
an open window

In the distance a church bell rings...

Translated by Will Firth

Path of no return

I am seeking the way
to my old house
I will live there through
the snowy winters
and the autumn rains
I will endure
the blazing heat of summer
the starkness of the mountains
and the black web of loneliness
just to be sure
that the old house
still rings to childhood's chatter
and grandfather's tales.

Translated by Will Firth

Zvonko Taneski

Room

Why didn't they let me change the room
and make me feel better,
now that even the critics are allowed to change their views
and earn more space in the magazines?

They all went for large and bright rooms
with evidently functional furniture,
and I didn't even complain about the only one new, but hard armchair,
no trace of the second one, though there should've been a pair,
just like literature is inseparable from the science about it.

Why was I not standard guest when choosing the bed,
and was so resolute in my desire to experiment?

Literature needs fresh love masks for modelling:
a water-bed, an exotic partner with different skin colour, faith,
an unexpected adventure...

But not much depended on, I thought, what view the window had,
everything depended on where and who she'd look at
and who she'd recognize.
"Each room has a mirror", so I hope mine would have one too,
for it shouldn't, by any means, be an exception to the rule.

Why does my head look like a syntagmatic axis
though it is laid softly on the pillow,
and becomes a hypertext when it sinks in deep sleep?

Shouldn't they have let me change my room?

Translated by Zoran Ancevski.
English language editor: Lee Schweninger.

A good hunter

One, two and oops!

I'm falling asleep again,
I'm followed by fatigue everywhere,
it won't release the repose from its claws,
it won't allow me to sprout,
to open my eyes that shine like neon lights
with an expired date,
to palpate the world through the pulse of a neurotic
obliged to take a daily dose of opium
since he lacks a car to take him to infusion.

Two, three and down!

The tongue is fooling around with its forms,
with its function of a policeman on duty,
trying to examine my alimentary canal
how it swallows the grammatical rules:
as sweets, as chocolate, as a novel.

A bad game, muse!

No sooner have we got used to linguistic labour
than there go the men of letters with their fantasy –
to look for cracks in the tongue,
to deepen their imagination.

So is there now a volunteer to stop them in their search?

A good hunter, perchance?

Translated by Jovana Stojkovska

Darko Leshoski

Things worth living for, that I never read about in any damn textbook

It was worth living for these things:

The window cleaners who got dressed up as superheroes to amaze and delight those children in that oncology ward

The English grandad who saved over six hundred Jewish children from going to concentration camps and for fifty years only a handful of people knew about it

Woody Harrelson when he coolly gives the million dollars from that indecent proposal by that wanker Redford to an elephant or tiger or whatever it was at an auction and leaves with his hands in his pockets and a perverse smile

Last June when 12 Japanese surgeons knelt in front of an operating table after a hundred hour operation in which they were unable to save a nine-year-old child with cancer, who had decided to donate his healthy organs if he didn't survive the operation and they did just that after kneeling

Dennis Hopper when he holds up Christopher Walken with a ridiculous story in *True Romance* and spits blood as they beat him so that his son has more time to get further away

Isaac's face when he forgives his father for sacrificing him in the service of a God who nobody's ever seen

"Shoot if you want cousin, shoot!" and the ease with which that line is said when one's conscience is clean

Priam when he goes to see Achilles

When the old man goes to the strongest man in the world and goes like: "give me my son's body so I can bury him, you little piss-ant!"

Getting up in the middle of a wedding to catch a bus and go 200 km because she's got a temperature of 37.2

The hundred-year-old homeless man in Sofia who travels 50 km each way to beg, then secretly gives the money to orphanages and children

The bread factory after the 1963 Skopje earthquake – a donation from ... Ethiopia. Jesus Christ, the irony

My Uncle's hunger strike and the few against 20 million because of some fucking water and justice

The Swedish cops who helped that kid write his maths homework after he got scared that someone was breaking in and stayed with him until his mother came back from work

Nikola Tesla's coolness and benevolence

Kafka's letters

My Father breathing life into my Grandad as his soul was leaving him and his "your word is your bond" that makes a man

My Gran's "if they throw stones at you, you give them bread" – when I had no idea what she was talking about but now I understand

"If there is a God he will have to beg my forgiveness", inscribed on a wall at Treblinka

That Bosnian woman's letter to her kids (that bit telling her son to take off his socks before shagging, buy his girlfriend flowers and be good to her and he'll get everything he wants for the rest of his life)

My other Uncle's quietly serene silence like a cat purring even if there's a war going on outside

Drinking heavily with a total stranger you met at the bar an hour ago – until the break of day

That feeling that tells you that he might commit suicide or do something stupid because a terrible thing happened to him last night or a few hours ago

His tears and that morning's clutching embrace as if you had long ago stitched up a wound of his and hadn't seen him since

Kipling's *If*, every word of that poem

The covertly sent text to a girl: "You want me to say I'm going to the toilet and we get outta here?" at the packed out promotion of your first book

"For you, a thousand times over!" The last line from *Kite Runner* like an echo in Amir's ears

The smile of my high school teacher who never once had a go at me for being crap at maths cos she knew I had another gift

Sitting in the back of a cab with a bottle of vodka and gypsy music blaring having told the driver to just drive so that you don't go fuck someone up, even though he actually deserves it – until your rage subsides

The verses my Father wrote for my sister "all jewels will be worthless to me and already dwindle in the brilliance of your eyes" when she was little. The thought that I'm going to learn to teach other children to write with their hearts, not their heads!

My sister's brief knock knock on my door and the steaming cup of tea left waiting for me, because without saying a word she knows I'm not okay and can't even bear to see anyone

Those around me who know it all and have never left me in the mud

Vaptsarov's poem for his wife, which I could recite in my sleep:

"Sometimes I'll come when you're asleep
An unexpected visitor from afar...
Don't leave me outside in the street
From the door remove the bar!

I'll enter quietly, softly sit
And gaze upon you in the dark.
Then when my eyes have gazed their fill,
I'll kiss you and ... depart."

The last words of the three-year-old Syrian boy before he died/his death: Everything! I'm gonna tell God everything!

The scent of rekindled love you thought lost long ago

The scent of her skin

The thought that one day you'll be good, at least in part

At least a tad

And that nobody will find out.

71

how? in whose footsteps? and when?

see, you found yourself once

Until you're no more

Until you're no more

Life was thus far worth living for these things.

One day if I have a kid I'll tell him about these things when he's grown up a bit

I'll be telling him as we rip each and every page out of his textbooks if they're the same as today's and I'll teach him to make paper boats and planes

While schools grade only their heads and not their hearts

I'll tell him about Seagull beach and we'll release them through a dam on some river

Along the water

I'll also tell him the story of the boy who had the Sun on his left shoulder and the Moon on his right. He'll realise that boy truly existed – only after I'm gone.

Translated by Igor Stefanovski

"Shoot if you want cousin, shoot!" is from the final scene of the film, *Before the Rain*

IV Poetry & prose

Eli Krasniqi

Southern flower leaves

They rustle
Flower leaves in my room
Clamorous, they sound polyphonic to me
They aren't magnolias
As in Billy Holiday's *Strange Fruit*
But from the south they are
The south of my country

'Pastoral scene of the gallant south'
Sheep bells and horse trots
Dreams fleeing into the mountains
The roof cannot hold them

The blossoming flowers,
The sky is never theirs
Nor the roofs of the houses
Under them they stay and contemplate
The south of our country

Translated by Alexandra Channer

Poems of the garden

The building turned its back to the garden,
To the benches rotten from moist
Surrounded with trees, withered grey leaves
No insects to be seen, no dragonflies,
No light, but it is not cold
Catatonic she is
The dwellers come out in their windows, balconies
They put their clothes to dry, they take their dried clothes
They see her
They whisper
A reverberation is heard, perhaps birds
From other gardens
There are hedgehogs, no insects, nor butterflies
The noise of the city gathers here
Her shoulders are the roads that one cannot walk

It's getting dark, but the sky is still white
The hedgehog grey garden is breathing freely
After a wave of heat, a din of rain revived it
From the balconies, the dinging of spoons and plates is heard
Dinners are put on tables
She is catatonic
A bottle cork pulled her wheeze
The wine wet her feet
Her stomach is a vortex where words are killed

The light wakes up the garden
Smells like sage
She catches sunrises with her fingers
Like a needle that traverses
Undressed dresses
Catatonic she becomes
Snails move in her body
Leeches suck her life
Her head is an apiary
Her heart
Hollow of memories

Trees wake up the same
Sleep the same
– The garden of graves –
The lights penetrate them
Under the shade of a cherry tree
The longing does not die
Dad.

Translated by the author

A waltz

Here is a waltz for the lost loves
The tangerine aroma and the pain that drips
For our palms sweating from fear
For the emptiness whenever the memory frightens

Here is a waltz for the lost loves
And for those that we never lose.

Translated by the author

Zvonko Karanović

Notes from a cardboard church

Sometimes he saw how sea rises into the sun, or saw himself riding a bicycle in three foot deep water, or how he controls birds with his thoughts.

It wasn't that strange at all.

His job was to „have, visions" to write them down, and from time to time send them to those who didn't care about them at all.

He didn't consider himself a prophet nor a preacher.

Still, he built a church on top of a garbage container.

In the church, a cardboard box yellowed from the rain and sun, he received a mangy kitten.

It kept him company, while he often after midnight, lit up by candlelight, wrote letters to himself.

Days passed peacefully until the big incident caused by the sentence:

When we stay alone we must concentrate on our looks.

As soon as he put a period to his thought, magpies started to screech loudly on the gallows, the bats of conscience peeped.

From the dark depths he was whipped by an inner voice:

„Appearance is an illusion! Everything that exists is inside!"

Frightened, he wrote as if possessed:

The mode of existence... Negating superficiality... Life underneath the surface...

He remembered that he was writing to himself and that there's no need to defend his actions so he put down the pencil.

The mangy kitten raised its paw in the corner.

Attached to its chest as a badge, the tiny, neon Coca-Cola ad flickered in the darkness, and he realized that he was there for the completely wrong reasons.

Translated by Biljana B. Obradović

A sudden event in the museum of memories

He was sitting in a cheap, fake-leather armchair staring at the sign on the wall for a long time:
Man must try harder in order to be taken more seriously!
His eyes then fell on a wooden shelf with the dusty record player without a needle, broken for a while, the framed photograph of the smiling girl and the collection of poems, *A Season in Hell.*
He went into the kitchen and returned with a small hatchet.
First he broke the frame.
Then with a strong blow he flattened the plastic cover of the record player, threw the device on the floor and stomped on it wildly.
For a few moments he stared at the mess in front of him and grabbed the book from the case.
He didn't want to tear it apart immediately.
He went back to the armchair and slowly, sadistically, tore it page by page stopping from time to time to randomly read a line or two.
When he only had the cover in his hands, he looked up satisfied.
He was looking at the sign on the wall.
Outside the darkness thickened with a dull growl.
Inside the scattered things were creating a new, quite fresh and unexpected order.

Translated by Biljana B. Obradović

A late return home

Winter. Bark wrapped in ermine fur.
In a steam bath butterflies rise up from the naked shoulders.
Spread wings of easels and plaster sculptures.
An age of irony and hyper-irony.
It's cold.
Perhaps someone might bring some wood?
The story could continue with plenty of surprises.
A possibility has been named for two truths to replace one.
The Senate has approved of a budget rise in order to acquire
new and fresh mental images.
A machine for the conversion of memory into lyrical cadences
has remembered half an apple.
The wings didn't serve their purpose.
Balloons filled with sand first rose to the sky.
Disease has sneaked up and pulled away a victim.
The sick man manifested the character of a dog.
Winter. Long time ago.

Translated by Nataša Srdić

Krystalli Glyniadakis

A day of not so minor losses

This morning: a cat. A black
and white cat lying by the side of the road
as I was driving back and forth
between house and depot. He lay stock-
still with his feet stretched forth,
calm as if asleep. I pulled over,
crossed the road, gently picked him up.
He had grown stiff but his soft fur
asked to be caressed and combed.
I entered the yellow field behind him
and placed him under the cool
shadow of an aging olive tree,
as old as old people and as gentle. To rest
in a gentle land hit by reckless drivers.

Written in English

Letter from Moscow

My love,

In a bookstore, the other day,
Among thousands of books
And thousands of aluminium shelves,
Among the gleaming *babushkas* and flashy *cartes postales*
Behind the glass, protective cases
Of Parker pens and *tick-tack* clocks

I found a book
Where it was said that Stendhal learnt
How to write tersely
By reading and re-reading
Napoleon's field commands.

And that Descartes died of exhaustion
Having to wake up every day
For pre-dawn lessons in philosophy
To Queen Christina of Sweden

Who didn't like his dualism
Nor he, her other interests.

And that the corpses in World War I
Would reek of filth and lice, my love,
And pus and eczema and blood
Even if they did not belong to soldiers
        Or other combatants.

A man passed me by, the other day,
        My love,
On the street. He wore a sweater,
A heavy thing, a tattered, worn
Pistachio knit, with brown and grey lozenges;
A jacket, too, nylon-made
With nylon lining and nylon threads;
A pair of pants, the kind of pants
That stay pressed
And starched and beige.

I had just walked into the park of Cosmonauts
Under a blue, then green, then red hammer-and-sickle.
Behind my back, two giant, copper statues

– Workers, a he, a she –
Were lifting one colossal bale of hay
Ten meters high. Beneath their feet
Kids riding out
Their brand new bikes
With training wheels
And pink-glo helmets.

The man passed me by, my love,
On his way home   to his flaying flat
                        His ageless *kommunalka*
                        His iron train
                        His squealing bus
                        His thin-leafed book
                        His leather, knobbly armchair and his
                        yellowing lampshade

He passed me by
And on his shoulder he was carrying
                        The Cosmonauts
                        The bales of hay
                        The bicycles
                        The helmets and the books
                        The all-things nylon
                        And the battered, wooden escalators of the metro
                                that led deep, deep inside the earth
                        And the 13,000 volunteers from Komsomol
                                who dug it
                        The thousand tons of dirt they pushed up to the surface
                                in simple, hand-held carts and rusty rails.

I saw it in his eyes, my love,
When he passed me by
And looked at me, without seeing me
On his way to a book among millions of books among millions
of shelves among thousands of streets and thousands of men and
statues and hammers and sickles and escalator steps leading up to
exhausting dualism and down to terse commands.

Written in English
Sept 2016

Mircea Dan Duta

The cannibals

I fed on you,
for as long as there was something left to eat.
In fact, I somehow sensed
you would not be here for long.
Now they are eating me
And I have to be glad of it.
For as long as there is food for them,
It means I´m still here.
But you can no longer be aware of this.

Translated by Judit Antal and Bernie Higgins

The wave

I was coming out of Tesco's
and I saw her on the other side of the bridge.
She was as beautiful as ever.
I waved at her
and called her name: Cześć, Kasia.
But she kept going.
Maybe she didn't see me,
didn't hear me
or didn't understand me.
Or maybe in the realm of death
they just don't speak Polish.

Translated by Judit Antal and Bernie Higgins

Next stop

In the Paradise Garden there's no smoking,
no drinking,
no drugs,
Marys don't lose their virginity
and don't give birth in stables,
no names are taken in vain,
especially if no-one bears them,
no apple stealing,
no snake killing,
no Polish speaking
and no metro passing through.
And even if it did,
it certainly wouldn´t stop,
so in any case we should get off
at the next station.

Translated by Judit Antal and Bernie Higgins

Gazmend Krasniqi

The meeting

That man whose thoughts shout louder
than a convoy of cars; who at dusk-light drinks
the must of days that don't make history; who brings
no emotion nor deceiving reason; who brings
no distances traced on the back of the earth; that man
bears my name. His journey ends in an ancient book.

Or books that I never take from the shelves at least,
neither for a death nor for a celebration since
they don't resolve the ages' doubtful formulae.
So what's the point of meeting him after all, I wonder,
if he doesn't care about my cares or if the river doesn't flow upward,
and why I draw him wings or if the river doesn't sleep,
and why I sing him lullabies! So I wonder if this meeting-torture
might perhaps be the gateway to a new tyranny.

Translated by Granit Zela and Silvia Kadiu

Aesthetic hour

If a house of sun and rain
is built – as Cézanne once did –
with a cone, a cylinder and a sphere,
the Real would not be in ruins;
Beauty's Rainbow would come to drink
and rummage with gentle fists
through Eternity and Non-Being –
it's you who must become the Real,
a shape almost sunny, a mimosa flower,
the first on the balcony on a rainy day;
let's not walk or talk – may the time
between two frail space stations
be filled with this aesthetic hour.

Translated by Granit Zela and Silvia Kadiu

The materialist notes

In eager anxiety, could there be a fruitful end
to this dawn waning faintly like a frail flower
that's never known good fortune? Where
the Bohemian came and went, fast as a bullet
fired at long-winded delirious prophets,
without touching the day's coffee,
without buying the paper, in a popular bar,
behind the park, where the pigeons used to sit
and the waiter made courteous gestures?
Summer could come then – too late to dream
of enlightenment. The vice that drenched the heart
would come and I would think: these are just thoughts.
Somebody prayed to God to be more lonely.
Did I have ambition? Should I test fate?
Wearing old bills as a costume, I didn't know
who I was: would I know who I am
in the waiter's spurious smile? Here and there
the spirit, the things look like they've been distilled
for years – the metaphysical moment still irks you: here
I was. And when death comes for real and the dialectic
strikes again: the bread – has been bought;
shirts – to be ironed; the court decision – expected;
as a consequence – the cleaner and milkmaid.
You and I, earth and heaven – on this side
of the materialist notes' high fence,
where I collect coffee dregs one by one,
where I'm thankful for every heartbeat, where
with meagre hope I trace a path dazed by elusive splendour,
we're opening to each other forever and ever
until the very dirtiest of secret tasks.

Translated by Granit Zela and Silvia Kadiu

Filitsa Sofianou-Mullen

VI. (December flight)

The dawn will come brilliant
  and swift
    like midday in June
the giant bird will
  swoop down white and fierce
    unpredictable in its manoeuvres
those three who cannot hold their grip
  on its sleek snowy feathers
will fall down, down
  (one will be covered with a sheet
    by the curb
  another will be devoured
    by feral dogs with lions' manes
  the third will ask awed passers by
        Which one am I?)

Blagoevgrad, December 7, 2011

XV. (Christina 1979)

The third day is ushered in
   by the incessant call of cats
      in heat;
in the schoolyard, uniformed a rebellious blue,
   her friends will ask
      how can June be crueller than this book
        these pens and boards?
And who will speak of her tight black curls
   her skin so pale and radiant
   her always misty eyes
      (everyone's petard)
in a church so silent with sobs?

That same night a girl will smell her mother's
   musky hair and wonder what smells
      outrage the grave.
Embraced like this
   – one earth in two –
they will construe
   the cats' insistent calls
   and spread their laughter, muffled,
      on the still wet pillow.

Thessaloniki, January 12, 2012

'VI. (December Flight)' and 'XV. (Christina 1979)' appear in the English version of *Prophetikon* published by Scalino in Sofia, 2014.

Vukan Mihailović de Deo

We awake at night

We awake at night
On soft earth
On our knees.

Pure in his coming
He raises his injured
Palm before me.

He bestows on me the peace
Of his revealed body –
I wipe my lips and gaze.

Thoughts are like circles
Around slumbering days
Around unnoticed smiles.

The time
Within our longing
Grows.

Translated by Will Firth

An open wave

He stands wet at the brink,
Looks at me and frowns:
This child is an open wave.

He is the sound of my summer thoughts.

My cheeks hurt as I smile
To myself as a boy and as man in defeat:
They grow in the near afternoon.

I know – his body is a kiss,
His desires quarrel over his hair;
I see – time is full of tenderness.

And I am quiet
As the shoulders of childhood leave,
Soft blades of the day.

Translated by Will Firth

In the winter light

I see no faces in the winter light,
I see no children or lovers,
But the windows look festive:
Yellow pictures in clean buildings,
Distant voices in peaceful rooms.

I think only of winter in the streets,
In the transparent turning of the stars.

On the footpaths, like white apparitions,
A hand reaches out for young bodies –
Their eyes are dark fish in motion:
They roam the squares
They do not recognise me.

Translated by Will Firth

Essay: Passion and coincidence

When it comes to contemporary literature from SE Europe, the number of books translated into English in any one year is miniscule. While publishers and booksellers report what they describe – somewhat optimistically – as a "boom" in the sales of translated fiction, any upsurge is largely accounted for by a relatively small clutch of best-selling novels – those by Elena Ferrante, for example, or the 'Scandinoir' school. In UK bookshops, the only works by Balkan writers you're likely to find readily available are the novels of Orhan Pamuk from Turkey and Ismail Kadare from Albania. This, of course, is a good start. Both Pamuk and Kadare are undoubtedly major literary figures, not only in their own countries, but in the world as a whole and fully deserve the list of international accolades that each of them has accrued.

The translations of their work, though, are very much the tip of the proverbial iceberg and it only takes the briefest of visits to any bookshop in a SE European country to realise quite how much contemporary writing *isn't* being translated into English – and quite how much contemporary English-language writing is being translated into SE European languages, for that matter. It is, after all, much easier to find a copy of *Game of Thrones* translated into Bulgarian than it is to find a book of poems by a Bulgarian poet translated into English.

This article, though, isn't intended to be a prolonged whinge about the lack of translations of Balkan literature in general and of Balkan poetry in particular. While the debate around why such a lack exists is an interesting one, it's more useful to focus on what actually is available in translation and offer pointers to those who'd like to read more work from the region. The following won't be a comprehensive survey and there are bound to be publications which have passed me by, but I can at least mention some of the things which are out there and which I've come across during late-night online trawls or chance conversations.

As I've said, on the prose fiction side of things, Kadare and Pamuk are there, on the shelves in actual bookshops – although, in Kadare's case, what's been translated is, in itself, a relatively small proportion of the work of a hugely prolific writer. That immediately becomes obvious when you go into the International Bookshop on Skanderbeg Square in the Albanian capital, Tirana. While in the UK the translations of his novels and novellas might at best fill a few inches of shelf space, in Tirana his books fill entire bookcases and encompass essays, short stories, plays and poetry as well as his longer fiction. Having left Albania in 1990, shortly before the final collapse of the communist regime, Kadare spends much of his time in Paris and a French translation of his complete works – complete but for his essays – has been published by Fayard. As many of the novels have been translated into English from French rather than Albanian, perhaps this will lead to a greater range of his work being translated, including the poetry.

That said, some of Kadare's poems have been translated by Robert Elsie and published on his Albanian literature website. For those interested in Albanian poetry, in fact, Elsie's website – www.albanianliterature.net – is an invaluable resource, being an extensive collection of work which incorporates oral epic verse and the poetry of the nineteenth-century *Rilindja* or national revival as well as that of contemporary poets from Albania itself, the Albanian-speaking communities of Kosova, Macedonia and Montenegro and the Arbëresh-speaking Italo-Albanian community in southern Italy. As you'd expect of a collection covering such a vast scope, the poetry itself is hugely diverse, ranging from the highly rhythmical epic narratives of "the songs of the frontier warriors" to the recognisably modernist and post-modernist work of contemporary poets such as Arian Leka, Luljeta Lleshanaku and Ervin Hatibi.

Elsie's books, meanwhile, include a translation – with the Canadian poet Janice Mathie-Heck – of Gjergj Fishta's monumental 'national epic' *The Highland Lute;* the 2008 anthology of Albanian poetry *Lightning from the Depths*, which has a similarly extensive scope to the website and is a joint work with Mathie-Heck; and, more recently, *Under the Banners of Melancholy*, the collected literary works of Albania's most influential 20th-century poet Migjeni. Born in 1911, Migjeni is generally credited with having introduced modernism into Albanian literary culture, moving away from the patriotic pastoralism of the *Rilindja* poets and towards a social realism which, in its declarative style and its chronicling of the effects of poverty, recalls the work of Brecht. Although he published little in his own, brief lifetime (he died in 1938), Migjeni undoubtedly remains a key figure and the publication of *Under the Banners of Melancholy* is a major step in the slow but steady uncovering of Albanian poetry in English.

Start looking for SE European poetry in translation, in fact, and you might be forgiven for thinking that those who bemoan its absence aren't Googling diligently enough. There are, for example, relatively recently published country-specific anthologies of poetry from most of the SE European countries. Perhaps the most well-known – and most urgent – of these is Penguin's *Austerity Measures*, published in March 2016. Edited by Karen Van Dyck, it's an anthology of Greek poetry, most of which has been written since 2008's financial crash and much of which responds – directly, obliquely or otherwise – to the impact of the economic crisis. This has certainly been reviewed very positively – "the anthology excites partly because (in refreshing contrast to much of what one reads in English) so many of these poems needed to be written," said Kate Kellaway in the Guardian – and even prompted claims that, despite or perhaps even because of its recent misfortunes, Greece is undergoing a cultural renaissance. Whether true or not, such claims do at least help to raise the profile of contemporary Greek writing.

With a bit more sleuthing, you might also come across others from this group of country-specific anthologies. Also published in 2016, the enigmatically titled *Cat Painters* is the most comprehensive anthology of Serbian poetry published in English since Charles Simic's *The Horse has Six Legs* in the USA back in 1992 and features the work of more than 70 poets from the generation born in the 1960s onwards. There's a good and wide-ranging selection of Romanian poetry in 2006's *Born in Utopia* – which delves back through the 20th century to Paul Celan and Tristan Tzara (both of whose Romanian origins are often occluded by their subsequent careers) – while the slightly older *Scar on the Stone* from 1998 anthologises the work of 14 Bosnian poets and prompted Adam Piette to write in *Translation and Literature* that: "In gathering the voices of witnesses to the terrible war, the vicious days of Sarajevo, [editor Chris] Agee produced an invaluable set of documents about the impact of history on ordinary citizen imaginations, even into the hell of Omarska."

A more recent addition to this small but important corpus of translated poetry is Christopher Buxton's 2016 anthology *Flowers Don't Grow Singly*, a collection of classic Bulgarian poetry which includes work by some of the most important Bulgarian poets from the nineteenth and early twentieth centuries, from Hristo Botev and Peyo Yavorov to Geo Milev and Nikola Vaptsarov. Strictly speaking, perhaps, this isn't an anthology of 'contemporary' poetry (although that depends very much on how you define the term), but serves as an illuminating introduction to what has followed in the burgeoning Bulgarian poetry scene – a taste of which can be had from two other anthologies: *At The End of The World* from 2012 and *The Season of Delicate Hunger* from 2014. Published in the UK and USA respectively, these both contain many of the most engaging and important poets to have emerged in Bulgaria both during and after the end of the socialist period, including some of those featured in this issue of *Balkan Poetry Today*.

A somewhat less conventional anthology comes in the form of *A Balkan Exchange* from 2007. Edited by W.N. Herbert, this is a bespoke anthology in the sense that, in its editor's words, it "maps a singular encounter between two groups of poets, one based in the Bulgarian capital Sofia, the other in the North East of England." In short, over the course of four years, four poets in Sofia – Kristin Dimitrova, Georgi Gospodinov, Nadya Radulova and VBV – collaborated with four British poets – Andy Croft, Linda France, W.N. Herbert and Mark Robinson – on both translations of each other's work and original poetry inspired by their exchange. The result is a book which goes beyond translation and brings genuine cross-cultural dialogue to the page with, for example, Mark Robinson's 'Eleven Attempts at an Explanation' and Georgi Gospodinov's 'Eleven Attempts at a Definition' being just one example of how such international conversations can work.

As it happens, *A Balkan Exchange* is published by Arc, long-term champions of poetry in translation and UK-based publishers of two other books with SE European connections: 2006's *Six Slovenian Poets* and 2011's *Six Macedonian Poets* – both of which afford a foothold in the appropriately mountainous volumes of Balkan poetry.

At the same time, of course, the internet has provided further opportunities for publishing SE European poetry in translation. Versopolis (**www.versopolis.com**) – based in Slovenia – and The Ofi Press (**www.ofipress.com/poetry**) – based in Mexico – both feature notable contributions from Balkan poets while Words Without Borders (**wordswithoutborders.org**) has also recently focused on Montenegrin and Bulgarian writers.

The paradox here, of course, is that in mentioning these anthologies and online ventures, I appear to be describing what might be described as – well, yes – a boom. I haven't even mentioned the novels by Balkan poets like Marija Knežević from Serbia being published by Istros Books or the Oscar nomination for the short animation *Blind Vyasha* based on a story by Georgi Gospodinov from Bulgaria or, indeed, the translations of the latter's two novels which have been published in the USA, *Natural Novel* and *The Physics of Sorrow*.

That said, the proportion of writing from SE Europe available in English translation remains relatively small – one might even say tiny – and many of the books and projects mentioned here are the result of either chance encounters or personal enthusiasms. Yes, there are organisations and funding bodies which support translation and exchange and these have played an essential role in bringing projects to fruition, but often as not it's passion and coincidence which have led to individuals initiating such projects in the first place. Thankfully, the results to date of this rather ad hoc arrangement can at least offer a glimpse of the wealth of new writing going on in the Balkans and will hopefully lead to further collaboration, translation and exchange in future.

Tom Phillips

Arian Leka

From *Sea Book*

March

I

Locked.
Slow.
And pregnant.

Broken piers. Twisted masts
thrust deep into the ship's head
before crucifixes surface in dreams.

The streets tumble, stabbed in the back by the wind.
The mind returns to a night in Epidamnus.
The memory's seared with salt, picks myrtle flowers.

People hobble themselves against growing up fast
and leaving for heaven where names are woven in white thread
and the stitches can hardly be seen.

Sweet and sour you were, oh sea.

– Am I your king? I waited for the words to reach your ears.
– Yes, you are, but show yourself, make peace, be silent,
you said in a monotone voice, tired of me, of yourself
and of those who resemble us.

March had come for the earth on shore.

Flowers bloom on the hills
waves in the sea.

Translated by Suadela Balliu and Silvia Kadiu

From *Correcting Mistakes*

XVI [Love in autumn is an ill-starred plant]

Love in autumn is an ill-starred plant.
Its fruits grow buried in the dark.
Its flowers don't live long, nor do its leaves.

Simple children unblessed,
come by day, gone by night,
baptized with mud and black water.

The body in this season is more longing than languid.
It takes on the shape of a darning needle.
It enters and exits your body
simply to sew a small flower.

A simple flower.

Sewn with white thread
without a knot or hitch.

Flowers are creatures without stitches.

It's the same effort almost.

It's almost the same effort the mind needs
to steer a sail towards simple paths
where the word *want* dies for the word *must*
and they're often wasted
sacrificed
in each other's place.

Love in autumn was an ill-starred plant.
Fruit, flower and leaf
from which
the green fades without leaving a trace.

And where I,
in the only shape remaining to me,
that of the darning needle with an eye,
have to enter your weary body

to stitch
all that I unstitched

and all that I found unstitched
in you.

Translated by Suadela Balliu and Silvia Kadiu

Slađana Kavarić

A feeling of total life. Opposition to the conscious world.
Attempting to see the gulf
between feelings that exclude each other.
You radiate, as if your mouth harboured a solar structure,
you take your place in the cosmos,
and my hands drag my right leg out of chaos.
When light damns the nausea, nonchalance will bask, in twosomeness.
Opposition to the real world. A numbing feeling in ambivalence.
The coming light, outstretched arms and a sigh, from within.
I wish my arms were spread like curtains. In the breeze.

Translated by Will Firth

All those who cry, cry in boredom or over Tarkovsky.
You decay for much longer that you breathed air,
drew with clammy fingers on the fogged-up window,
held your head bowed and screamed that you recognised a voice.

People don't look for you any more, now that going missing is no excuse.
With an open world above me, the derelict future reeks of a slow death
by my own sentence, on my legs.

I decrypt the pacific dullness you emit although you blink, posthumously.

Then I remember the big bags that swayed in the wind with the
lightness of your bones,
but they vanished, in crimson and sweat, in oblivion, in waking, in
disagreement,
while you kept explaining that you hate musicals because you are
made of drama and thrillers.

You were always ground down by nostalgia, you sliced off shreds of
memory,
and realised that you no longer have memories, that you are a statue
and only I recognise
the colour of your eyes.
They dropped you and you fell down dead, imploring, but staunchly
not waving your arms.
Your lips trembled, fragments of the past sang like a choir, but no
one was listening.
In the REM phase.

Translated by Will Firth

I am a real sea-wave
that is never calm and peaceful.
I am a quiet voice that always drowns out
all the loud and crude others.
My heart is large, but no path leads to it.
My soul is a beast
and growls at all that is not bestial.

Translated by Will Firth

Marko Pogačar

Man dines in his father's slippers

What used to be the borders now are you.
It was May, deep and flat,
the street gutted with roadwork, the snow
sudden, dry.
To be frank:
I didn't owe anyone anything.
I stood by the doorposts, the water
frozen by fear soaked my back.
And when I closed my eyes I saw
popcorn rush toward its salt and I knew
some nights the kernels blacken, like droppings.
I entered to face the sickening scene:
not love, stupidity, stupidity is the heart of the world –
and now in those slippers I eat and cry,
only eat and cry in the house.

Translated by Andrea Jurjević

Scabs

The afternoon decays on its wobbly legs,
thaws, a calf that won't make it to the butcher,
a pasture bathed in bellows, it all
gathers in an evening awareness, dim
and self-admitted: cots on low branches,
blood on grass blades, only traces
of horns, like everyday poison; teeth strewn
over the dangerous district of the mouth.

I'm trying out the logic of small moves,
I observe: light is the measure for all things.
properly carved pumpkins,
cans open to an infinite encounter,
coated with rust that braces door handles, offers
a view on the mechanism of earth, its scabs,
arranged across the window sill.

it's hard to tell what begins. the light that crawls
along interior walls lays silent April shadows
pumpkins bloom, rust peels off: can winter with its
teeth crush stamens, and the pasture thaws under hoofs;
a calf rises, shakes off the drool, its muzzle
takes in the damp air; decaying, it seems, is finished.

now truly, from some dusty files,
the night descends on the sky: it slips it on like favourite shoes.
first left then the right one, then laces, and the night is
at last stable. finally the night is at its home, in the sky,
in the throat of a calf: the darkness rustles in my ears,
in treetops that lean over us too closely –
the weight of the night presses; the stamp that inks the papers.

Translated by Andrea Jurjević

Ervina Halili

You, balloon

one day you'll fall to the ground
a deflated balloon in clumsy descent
if I find you slung on a lone branch
I'll grant you a fill of my breath till you're perfectly round
then tie you at the neck with a ribbon of peace
and watch as you rise, buoyed by my breath
all the way up to the jamboree in honour of coddled suns
where your arrival is awaited

Translated by Suzana Vuljević-Gojçaj

The same slumber

you've drifted off into the sleep of my death and you haven't woken
                                                            up from dreaming
it doesn't matter...
in wakeful reality
there are only eye-aches brought on from seeing the world
                                                        in slow-motion
vibrant hues from childhood surge upwards into an amorphous blur
and every other person is mad, floating about in his own balloon
small as he is
he lets out a sudden hair-raising cry
the clouds change course
rain
it's of no consequence...
a jazz melody sounds on metallic heads and waters the mushrooms
they multiply mercilessly over the surface layer of the head
there's no longer any hair there

you continue to sleep on the throne that reeks of cat urine
it doesn't matter...
who knows whose urine stench we inhale and whose decayed teeth
                                                    we chew each day
only now and then are we like blissful children riding on the backs
                                                            of dolphins
you...
coming from the gothic castle, your overcoat engulfed in spiders
in your gray-haired beard fluorescent corals grow
she...
bedaubed with the wax glaze of worries
she smiles dreamily, but rarely weeps
and so it goes...
rain...
silver cords drape over the hunched back in its saddle
freighted with logs of wood themselves laden with sorrow

once upon a time...
there was a man hanging by the neck from a rope, and his body
swayed timidly like a chunk of meat set to be paraded before
                                                    the butchers
a story of the flattened tires that have come to symbolize your life
tires that leave scuffmarks on asphalt still softened from the racket
                                                            of protest
I cannot bring the slogans back to mind

rain...
it's of no consequence...
I've forgiven you...

Translated by Suzana Vuljević-Gojçaj

Cats

the cats she paints have the expression of his face
when he opens his eyes in the morning

in the cats' bellies goldfish sail
a flowerbed glitters in the glow cast by the stars
and she is huddled into a ball

among the stars she says she constantly hears a sound preparing
                                                    to drop
to the ground
like a diamond summoning its strength to shatter

the next day he didn't return
she hung the cat paintings on the wall
like diamonds that will themselves shattered

Translated by Suzana Vuljević-Gojçaj

Stanka Nikač

The poem

It came out of nowhere
As if out of a dream
Like a winding brook from the forest
Through the wasteland
That knows the path

At dawn
Wells up into a well
Into the letters
Of a blessing

Translated by the author and Galina Tudyk

The muse behind the magic mountain

To the poet Dubravka Velašević

With music
The spear of the sky
To the sharp rhymes
Of the mountain
Down the rocks
Rolling the grains of sand
In the throat of the well

With music
The spear of the dragon
From the gorge
Of the black mountain
To the palace of jade
And of the ashes

The Muse
Behind the magic mountain
Threw the spear
Into your shell

Translated by the author and Galina Tudyk

Mentor Haliti

A view from the perspective of watercolours

O breath, you are nothing and everything, from that which made us and that which made the whole world, we try hard to catch you and hold you in our chests, the lovely scent of imagination, of heat, of sweat, of struggle, how it stinks, how to gasp, breath from what are you fleeing?
From the desert far away, from the dunes that encircle and flatten those who remain behind, while crushing and creating that wheaten flour from which the clay of the world was created. We'll make everything pitch black and arid up to the shore of the Mediterranean, out of watercolour.
The Mediterranean as dense as it seems is actually deeper, how did I fall into this monster that I remember, I don't know, in every direction I see a thin line that separates the sky and ocean, from the fish with a hook in its throat, and on my shoulders I carry a small body that still breathes, a soul that sways gently on the waves.
A storm will throw me into a beloved kingdom, far away from here, from this ocean which is saltier than the crystal sand, from this water that is harder than the air that doesn't let me weep, that tosses me around, that dissolves me, that turns me into salt, that makes my eyeballs swollen, I dream of fish, I see dolphins coming in societies, to play, to swim, to sprout wings in the coral.

Translated by Alexandra Channer

Grey filter

A bright colour bubbles in the rivers and blood vessels, you return to say how alive you are, how you want to stamp with your tiny shoe on each place in the world.
Oranges fall from the branches, swim like topaz seeds, the sky drowned in the evening.
The sweet sun rises yellow, like a scene drawn by a childish mind.
The leaves awake, the orchards are abundant, the green mountains flourish.
The sky, ocean, the sky above all else, all blue.
Aquamarine is the wound, violet sacrifice, ozone quilt.
The rose of the tree, the last tendril of a cluster of grapes mysterious eternity
Silence all around, a grey horizon, that filters into the mistletoe of blindness.

Translated by Alexandra Channer

Darling

Let me embrace you,
Let me kiss your feet,
Let me warm your hands,
We'll walk on the sand,
We'll play in the waves,
We'll light a fire,
We'll cook at night,
We'll vaporise the clouds,
We'll get drunk on seawater,
I'll let my spirit go to you,
So that you return to me again,
one love in my arms.

Translated by Alexandra Channer

Claudiu Komartin

Unfailing

I want to believe you when you say
someone will come
with a perfect smile
and unfailing gestures
an insect with the soul of a wet nurse
to push me on towards tomorrow
as you lead a horse crippled by sadness
at night   to the slaughter

Translated by Andrew K. Davidson

A spikey creature

I walked the streets all summer
with an obsession hard to name
and with the image of a child burning baby hedgehogs
at the borders of the clearing where
we walked naked and barefoot, knowing
love is a spikey creature
that will never again
come
home

Translated by Andrew K. Davidson

After Mom's visit

I don't know what brings people together any more.
(Another excuse to suffer?)

I hate to think of the future, when
someone spills blood under my words.

There's nothing noble about it, Sarah Kane.

And the sky endures, and the sky is spooled and whimpering.
A harvester slices ripe spires.

I sit and watch the things around
shrinking in diminished light.

Right here, a man and a woman yelled
at one another all night.

So much hatred in their eyes. I thought they'd kill each other.

There's nothing logical about it, doctor.

And now, stone by stone: aphasia.
No, it cannot go on. I am near.

Translated by Andrew K. Davidson

Notes on contributors

Jasmina Bolfek-Radovani (pen name Mina Ray) was born in Zagreb in 1965. She moved to London in 1995 where she has been living since. Jasmina has been writing poetry since 2014. She is especially interested in the experimentation with multilinguality in her writing. Her poems have been published in the UK literary journal *The Still Point Journal* (2015), the Croatian literary magazine *Tema* (2016) and the bilingual Canadian journal *Revue CMC* Review (2017).

Mircea Dan Duta is a poet, translator, film critic and theoretician born in 1967 in Romania, but of Czech expression and is considered today the only "Romanian poet of the Czech language" (other times as the only "Czech poet of Romanian origins"). He publishes his books in Prague, but also writes for Czech, Slovak and Romanian cultural reviews. Some of his works have been translated into Slovak, English, French, Hebrew, German, Polish and Romanian. Translations into Spanish are also expected soon.

Vukan de Deo was born in 1980 in Bela Crkva, Serbia. He studied comparative literature in Berlin and translation in Leipzig. He now lives and works in Berlin. His first book of poetry, *Behind the Window* (*Iza prozora*), is due to be published in Belgrade this year. He says of his writing: "My poems are not really political, they're more about provocation. If any political essence can be distilled at all, it's the idea that people should be free to choose the way they love, laugh and eat. I would be happy if my poems incited a rebellious *joie de vivre*."

The translator **Will Firth** was born in 1965 in Newcastle, Australia. He grew up mainly in Australia, punctuated by a formative three-year stay in Scotland and a student exchange to West Germany. Since 1991 he has been living in Berlin, where he works as a freelance translator of literature and the humanities (from Russian, Macedonian and all variants of Serbo-Croat). He is an Esperantist and a long-term participant in the anarchist movement. Firth occasionally translates poetry, but his main focus is on contemporary, socially critical prose from the countries of ex-Yugoslavia. See **www. willfirth.de.**

Krystalli Glyniadakis was born in Athens, Greece, in 1979. She's a bilingual poet, working in both Greek and English; she also works as a translator of Norwegian literature and as a rights manager in Greece's oldest publishing house, Hestia. She holds an MA in creative writing from the University of East Anglia, studying under George Szirtes and

Lavinia Greenlaw. Her three collections in Greek are all published by Polis Editions (Εκδόσεις Πόλις). She's been translated into Turkish and Slovenian and published, most recently, by Penguin and NYRB in Karen Van Dyck's *Austerity Measures: The New Greek Poetry*.

Ervina Halili was born in Kosova in 1986 and started to write poetry during the massive protest in Prishtina in 1997. She published her first poetry book at 17 while in 2015 she was awarded the national prize for poetry for the collection *Amulet*. Since 2012 she has travelled in different countries and experimented with new intermediate forms of literature and being itself. She published *Der schalf des Octous* in Vienna in 2016, and *Crowd 97* in Munich in 2017 while she was a resident at various literature houses in the Balkans and the rest of Europe.

Mentor Haliti was born in 1975 in Trnoc, Bujanovac. He studied dramaturgy in Prishtina and since 1999 has worked as a journalist on *Zëri* (*Voice*), *Lajm* (*News*), *Koha Ditore* (*Daily Times*) and *Express*. His publications include the poetry collections *Të thella janë rrënjët* (*Deep are the Roots*, 1996), *Shkallët e shtëpisë* (*House Stairs*, 2000), *Provokim* (*Provocation*, 2004) as well as works for theatre and comedy including *Caffe* (2008) and *Fabrika e kukullave* (*Puppet Factory*, 2009).

Dimana Ivanova was born in Varna, Bulgaria, in 1979. Her translations have been published in *Literary magazine, Panorama, Homo Bohemicus*, the *Anthology of young Czech authors translated by young Bulgarian translators* (2008). She is also the translator of several books from Czech and Slovakian and an author of a number of critical studies. She is the author of two books of poetry: *Invitation for a Father* (Ergo, 2012) and *Alphabet of the Desires* (Scalino, 2016). Her poems have been translated into English, Czech, Slovak, Spanish, Romanian, Russian, French and Macedonian and published in many journals in Bulgaria and abroad.

Jovica Ivanovski was born 1961 in Skopje, Macedonia. Recent poetry collections include: *Three Forward Three Backwards* (2004), *Double Album (In the Shadow of the Billboard and Ice-cream Infinitely)* (2005), *Siesta Thirst* (2007), *Whistling in the Wind* (2009), *With Straw in Mouth* (2011), *Morning Cinema* (2015), *The Sea is Up to My Knees* (2016), *A City that is No Longer Mine* (2016), as well as selected poems: *Open the Window and Let the City Breathe a Little*, (2002) and *One of These Days if Not Tomorrow* (2009). Jovica still lives and works in Skopje.

Zvonko Karanović is a poet and fiction writer born in 1959 in Niš, Serbia. He has published nine books of poetry and three novels. He has received several Serbian literary awards for poetry and an international fellowship from the Heinrich Boll Foundation (Cologne, Germany). His poems have been translated into 15 languages. His work has been published in many anthologies, most significantly in *New European Poets* (USA, Minnesota, 2008). His selected poems have been published in the USA: *It Was Easy to Set the Snow On Fire* (Phoneme media, Los Angeles, 2017). He lives in Belgrade as a freelance artist.

Slađana Kavarić is a Montenegrin author born in Podgorica in 1991. She writes poetry, short stories and articles on political culture. She has published two books of poetry: *Memory* (*Sjećanje*, 2010) and *People from Nowhere* (*Ljudi niotkuda*, 2016). Kavarić is particularly fond of Romanian writers, is fascinated by Germany and loves Joy Division and The Smiths. She doesn't believe in the dominant interpretations and trends of democracy and feminism, but rather in Andrei Tarkovsky's films and the future of the individual.

Marija Knežević is an award-winning poet, fiction writer, essayist, translator and professor of literature born in Belgrade, Serbia, in 1963. She has published more than 20 books including, most recently: *Shen* (poetry, 2011), *Fabula Rasa* (stories, 2012) and *Tehnika Disanja* (2015). Her 2005 novel *Ekaterini* has been translated into Russian, Polish, German and English and was described as "a terse, unconventional epic ... rich with detail and observation" in the *Central and East European Review*.

Claudiu Komartin was born in Bucharest in 1983. His first poetry collection, *Păpușarul și alte insomnii* (*The Puppeteer and Other Insomnia*, 2003, 2007) won the Mihai Eminescu National Award. He also published *Circul Domestic* (*Domestic Circus*, 2005), which was awarded The Romanian Academy Poetry Prize, *Un Anotimp în Berceni* (*A Season in Berceni*, 2009, 2010) and *Cobalt* (2013). He is co-author of two plays and editor of several anthologies of Romanian contemporary poetry. His work has been translated into German, Serbian, Bulgarian and Turkish. He is editor-in-chief of Poesis International literary magazine and is a member of Romanian PEN.

Elife (Eli) Krasniqi is an anthropologist, feminist activist and writer. She is a PhD candidate in SE history and anthropology at the University of Graz, Austria. She is a founder and director of Alter Habitus – a feminist institute for studies in society and culture in Prishtina. Her literary work has been published in Kosova and Albania. Her play *Citycide* will be published in May 2017 by Multimedia Centre, Prishtina.

Gazmend Krasniqi was born in Shkodra and lives in Tirana, Albania. He is a writer, essayist, anthologist and literary historian. His poetry collections include: *Në Kryqin e Dashurisë* (*At the Cross-roads of Love*), *Skodrinon* (*Skodrinon*), *Poema* (*Poems*); *Toka e (Pa) premtuar* (*The (Un)promised Land*), *Fletorja e Poemave* (*The Note-book of Poems*). His work has also appeared in a number of anthol-ogies internationally. In addition to poetry and prose, Krasniqi also writes for the theatre.

Mila Lambovska was born on 21 December, the day of the winter solstice. She graduated from St Kliment Ohridski University of So-fia with a Master's degree in clinical and consultative psychology. Working with people inspires her. She utilizes her experience in her consultative practice as a psychologist as well as in psychological astrology in her close cooperation with authors as an editor of lit-erary works. Her latest poetry collection, *The Year of Georgia*, was published by Scalino in Sofia at the end of 2016.

Arian Leka was born in 1966 in Durrës, Albania, where he attended music school. He studied Albanian language and literature in Tirana and modern literature in Florence. He is founder of the international poetry festival Poeteka and is editor-in-chief of the quarterly poetry journal *Poeteka*. His many publications include novels, short stories and collections of poetry, including *The Ship of Sleep* and *Strabismus*. His work has been translated into German, French, Italian, English, Spanish, Romanian, Bulgarian and Croatian.

Darko Leshoski was born on 4 July 1984 in Struga, Macedonia. His poems were known, read and shared by a wide public on social net-works and websites even before they were published in a book. In 2012, the well-known Macedonian magazine *Fokus* and Tea Moderna declared him as "one of the three faces that marked 2012" – together with Macedonian actor Nikola Ristanovski and Macedonian musi-cian Kiril Dzajkovski. His poems have been translated into English, Chinese, Slovenian and German.

Vladimir Levchev was born in 1957 in Sofia, Bulgaria and teaches literature and creative writing at the American University in Blago-evgrad. Between 1994 and 2007, he lived, studied and taught in the USA before returning to Sofia. A writer, critic and translator, he has published a novel, books of essays and poetry collections including 2004's *Black Book of the Endangered Species* (in the USA) and 2015's *Любов на площада* (*Love in the Square*, Scalino) which brings to-gether poems on love and politics written across several decades.

Amelia Licheva is a professor of literary theory at St Kliment Ohrid-ski University in Sofia, Bulgaria. Her recent poetry collections in-clude: *Азбуки* (*Alphabet*, 2002), *Моите Европи* (*My Europes*, 2007) and *Трябва да се види* (*Must Be Seen*, 2013). Her poems have been translated into French, German, Italian, Spanish, Polish, Slovak, Croatian and Hungarian. She is editor of *Литературен вестник* (*The Literary Gazette*) and *Литературата* (*Literature*) magazine. She was awarded the Рицар на книгата award in 2016 and Почетния знак на София (The Insignia of Honour of Sofia).

Iliyan Lyubomirov was born in 1990. He grew up in Sofia in Bulgaria before studying political science in Berlin. He co-founded the online literary project *Letters of Flesh* before publishing his first volume of poetry, *Нощта е Действие* (*The Night is Action*), in 2014. His second volume, *Лято* (*Summer*) followed in 2016. His work has received and been nominated for a number of national awards and he is currently engaged in a variety of projects involving poetry and creative writing.

Aksinia Mihaylova (1963) is a poet and translator living and working in Sofia, Bulgaria. She is co-founder of the literary magazine *Ah, Maria* and the author of six poetry collections including: *The Lowest Layer of the Sky* (2008), *Unbuttoning of the Body* (2011), which received the Hristo Fotev National Award for Poetry and the Milosh Ziapkov National Literary Award, and *Changing Mirrors* (2015), which won the Ivan Nikolov National Prize. She also writes in French and her poetry collection *Ciel à Perdre* (*A Sky to Lose*, 2014) received the Prix Guillaume Apollinaire. Mihaylova has translated over 35 books and her own poems have been translated into more than 17 European languages and published in the USA, Canada, Turkey, Egypt, Japan, China. Her selected poems have been published in Slovak, Arabic and Italian.

Stanka Nikač was born in Godinje, Montenegro, on the shores of Lake Skadar. A doctor by profession, she completed her medical training in Belgrade where she specialized in neuropsychiatry. Her first book of poetry, *Sonet maloj sobi* (*Sonnet to a small room*) was published in Podgorica in 2016.

Marko Pogačar was born in 1984 in Split, Yugoslavia (now Croatia). He has published nine books of poetry, essays and prose. In 2014 he edited the *Young Croatian Lyric* anthology. He is an editor of the literary magazine *Quorum* and of *Zarez*, a bi-weekly for cultural and social issues, and a literary critic for various newspapers and magazines. He has been a fellow of Civitella Ranieri, Literarische Colloquium Berlin, Récollets-Paris, Passa Porta, Milo Dor, Brandenburger Tor, Internationales Haus der Autoren Graz, Literaturhaus NÖ, and Krokodil Beograd. His poems have appeared in more than 30 languages.

Dušan Ristevski was born in Bitola, Macedonia in 1954 and migrated to Sydney in 1973. He has been actively involved in the community welfare field. Ristevski was a founding member of the Macedonian Literary Association 'Grigor Prlichev' and is also a member of the Macedonian Writers Association and the Macedonian Association of Journalists. He is an active playwright highly regarded in the Macedonian community in Australia and beyond. He has a number of books of poetry to his name, the latest being *Fear and Shame* (2006).

Alexander Shurbanov (Sofia, Bulgaria, 1941) has published 10 volumes of poetry and four collections of essays. His latest collection, combining the two genres under the title *Opit* (*Experience*), appeared last winter. He is the Bulgarian translator of Chaucer's *The Canterbury Tales*, Milton's *Paradise Lost*, Coleridge and Dylan Thomas as well as of Shakespeare's mature tragedies. For over four decades he has taught English literature at Sofia University and is the winner of a number of prestigious awards as a writer, translator and scholar.

Filitsa Sofianou-Mullen was born Stuttgart, Germany in 1962 and was raised in Kalamaria, Greece. She moved to Kent, Ohio in 1984 to attend Kent State University. She has been teaching writing and literature at the American University in Blagoevgrad since 2004. She is a poet, essayist, translator, who writes in English and Greek. Her 'poetic journal' *Prophetikon* was published in English and Bulgarian by Scalino, Sofia in 2014.

Ragip Sylaj was born in Sllapuzhan village of Suhareka commune in Kosova in 1959. His writing first appeared in the literary press in the late 1970s. He has worked as a teacher and as a journalist and editor on the students' newspaper *Bota e re* (*New World*) and the daily newspapers *Bota Sot* (*World Today*) and *Zëri* (*Voice*) in Prishtina. He currently works as a senior officer in the press department of the Kosovan Ministry of Foreign Affairs. He writes poems, prose, drama, essays and literary reviews.

Zvonko Taneski was born in 1980 and is a Macedonian poet, literary critic, translator and university professor living and working in Slovakia. He is the author of six books of poetry: *Opened Doors* (Kuboa, 1995), *The Choir of Rotten Leaves* (Matica makedonska, 2000), *The Ridge* (Magor, 2003), *Chocolate in Portfolio* (Blesok, 2010), *Necking without Warranty Card* (Kočo Racin, 2012) and *Waiting History* (Antolog, 2016). His poems have been translated into numerous languages and published in national literary periodicals as well as abroad.

Petar Tchouhov was born in 1961 in Sofia, Bulgaria. He has published 10 collections of poetry, a novel, a collection of short stories and a children's book. His work has been translated into 18 languages and included in many newspapers, journals and various anthologies in Bulgaria and abroad. He plays guitar in rock bands, writes music and lyrics. Petar has performed his poetry and music at festivals and other events in Japan, USA, Russia, Switzerland, Germany, Hungary, Croatia, Lithuania, Romania, Slovakia, and Macedonia.

Stevan Tontić was born in 1946 near Sanski Most, Bosnia-Herzegovina. He is a poet, prose writer, essayist and translator and has published 10 collections of poetry, of which the most recent are *Sveto i prokleto* (*Holiness and Damnation*, 2009) and *Svakodnevni smak svijeta* (*Everyday's End of the World*, 2013). He is the author of the novel *Tvoje srce, zeko* (*Your Heart, Bunny*, 1998), the anthology *Novije pjesništvo Bosne i Hercegovine* (*Contemporany Poetry of Bosnia-Herzegovina*, 1990) and *Moderno srpsko pjesništvo* (*Contemporany Serbian Poetry*, 1991). His work has been translated into numerous languages and has won both national and international literary awards.

Ivan Trposki was born in 1942 in Volino in Macedonia. He migrated to Australia in 1968 and settled in Sydney, where he worked on the railways for many years. His poetry has been published in the Australian-Macedonian press and in Macedonia itself, beginning with poems in the anthology *Vistas* (1984) and his own first book, *Shallow Roots* (1985). Trposki joined the Macedonian Literary Association 'Grigor Prlichev' in Sydney in 1979. He is a member of the Macedonian Writers Association and the Macedonian Association of Journalists, and writes regularly for the Macedonian press in Australia.

Suzana Vuljević-Gojçaj is a PhD candidate in history and comparative literature & society (ICLS) at Columbia University. Her dissertation reconstructs the transnational networks of a largely forgotten elite group of intellectuals that coalesced around pan-Balkanist initiatives in interwar South East Europe. Suzana holds a BA in history and comparative literature from the University of Michigan, Ann Arbor. She translates poetry and short prose from Bosnian/Croatian/Serbian (BCS) and Albanian to English.

Neşe Yaşın was born in 1959 in Cyprus. She is a poet well known and read on both sides of divided Cyprus. Her poem '*Which Half?*' – written at the age of 17 – has become an unofficial anthem for a united Cyprus. She has published eight volumes of poetry, one novel and a research book on literature. Selections from her poetry have been translated into more than 30 languages and published in magazines and anthologies internationally. A selection of her poems has been published in English translation with the title *Rose Falling Into Night*. She has participated in poetry festivals and readings around the world. She received the Anthias Pierides Award in 1998.

We hope you've enjoyed the very first edition of our newest venture *Balkan Poetry Today 2017*...

It was inspired by our other annual poetry magazine *Turkish Poetry Today* bringing the very best of Turkey's remarkable literary past and present to an English reading world...

As well as poetry we also publish fiction, translations, travel and history at Red Hand Books so please go to our website at :

www.redhandbooks.co.uk

to find out more and support independent publishers and booksellers.

Thank you for your support.
Everyone at Red Hand Books

red hand
B O O K S

www.ingramcontent.com/pod-product-compliance
Lightning Source LLC
Chambersburg PA
CBHW060019050426
42448CB00012B/2815